Johannes Brahms

OP. 122

Eleven Chorale Preludes for the Organ

Edited by
John E. West

G. SCHIRMER, Inc.

DISTRIBUTED BY

HAL•LEONARD®
CORPORATION

7777 W. BLUEMOUND RD. P.O. BOX 13819 MILWAUKEE, WI 53213

Contents

Note

These Eleven Chorale Preludes were composed by Brahms at Ischl, Upper Austria, in May and June, 1896, during the last year of his life, and were the only compositions by him issued posthumously.

In the present edition the notes for right and left hands have been clearly differentiated, either by re-staving where convenient, or by the indications *R.H.* and *L.H.*, and Brahms's use of the Alto Clef in certain passages has been discarded.

The time indications, dynamic marks, etc., given in the original edition have been retained, but all suggested modifications of these, or additions to them, will be found enclosed in brackets. In the more expressive passages a number of Swell pedal *crescendos* and *diminuendos* will suggest themselves to experienced players. It has been considered unadvisable, however, to add these and other details which are best left to the discretion of the performer.

Changes of manual formerly indicated as *Man. I.*, *Man. II.*, etc., have here been translated into suggested terms of *Gt.*, *Ch.*, *Sw.*, etc., but the choice of stops is left to the player, except in a few specific cases. One or two slight alterations have been made in the *place* of a manual change, for the sake of a better effect. Further suggestions have been made incidentally by means of foot-notes.

The somewhat intermittent use of phrasing slurs has been left almost entirely as given in the original. A few of them have been slightly modified in length and others have been added here and there in order to be consistent. It must be assumed, however, that the discontinuance of slurs by no means indicates that the music ceases to be *legato*.

English translations of the German texts of the Chorales have been provided.

John E. West

Eleven Chorale Preludes

Edited by
John E. West

Johannes Brahms, Op. 122, Book I

No. 1. Mein Jesu, der du mich
My Jesus calls to me

6

loud   the   Bride - - groom's
gro - - ssen   Bräut' - - gams

praise,
Ruhm

f (add)

In
so

(increase gradually)

The
gern
re
cr
joi
zah
ces
let

(rit. poco a poco al fine)

(ff)

- ces. [Trs. M.D. Calvocoressi]
- let.

No. 2. Herzliebster Jesu
O Blessed Jesu

No. 3. O Welt, ich muss dich lassen

O world, I now must leave thee

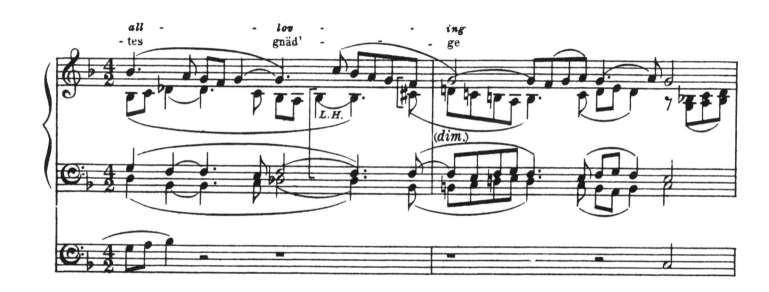

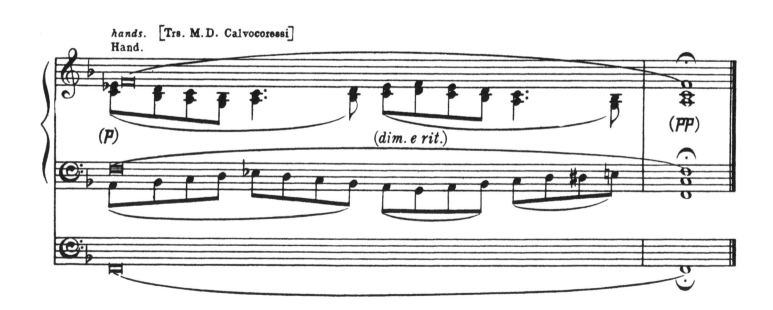

No.4. Herzlich thut mich erfreuen

My faithful heart rejoices

Heav'n and Earth in splen - dour Will He a - fresh cre -
Him - mel und die Er - den wird Gott neu schaf - fen

- ate, Sw.
gar,

Ch. (or Sw.)

And all of us, His
all Cre - a - tur soll

f Gt.

crea - tures, Shall pure and flaw - less be. [Trs. M.D. Calvocoressi]
wer - den ganz herr - lich, hübsch und klar.

(rit.)

No. 5. Schmücke dich, O liebe Seele

Deck thyself, my soul

Johannes Brahms, Op. 122, Book 2

[Trs. Catherine Winkworth]

(rit.)

No. 6. O wie selig seid ihr doch, ihr Frommen

Blessed are ye faithful souls

24

No. 7. O Gott, du frommer Gott

O God, Thou faithful God

gifts be - stow - - ing,
al - les ha - - ben,

(m)f Gt.

pure and health - y frame
- sun den Leib gib mir

(m)f Gt.

give me, and with - in
dass in sol chem Leib

(Gt.)
(Sw.)
(Gt.) (Sw.) (m)f Ch.

* The last R.H. note (E) on Gt. had better be omitted in performance.
† These two lines of the Chorale may be played on the Swell if preferred.

No. 8. Es ist ein' Ros' entsprungen

Behold, a rose is blooming

- mid the gloom of win - - ter Burst
- ten im kal - - ten Win - - ter wohl

forth in wond - - 'rous bloom. [Trs. M. D. Calvocoressi]
zu der hal - - ben Nacht.

Sw.

(rit.)

No. 9. Herzlich thut mich verlangen

My heart is filled with longing

(1st SETTING)

No. 10. Herzlich thut mich verlangen

My heart is filled with longing

(2nd SETTING)

End,
peace;

weil
For

ich
woes

hie
are

bin
round

um —
me

- fan — — — — gen
throng — — — — ing,

mit
And

Trüb — — sal
tri — — als

und
will

E —
not

p G! (soft 8 ft. stop)

-lend.
cease.

Ich
Oh

hab Lust ab - zu - schei - - - den von
fain would I be hast - - ing From

die - - ser ar - gen Welt,
thee, dark world of gloom,

(poco riten.)

(a tempo)

Sw. (━━━)

più dolce sempre

sehn'
To

* Changes of manual are indicated at these points in the original Edition, but the manual parts may be played throughout on the Swell
If preferred. In the latter case the suggested modification of phrasing given in dotted lines will be unnecessary.

mich   nach   ew' - - - gen
glad - - - ness ev - - - er -

Freu - - - - - den,   o
- last - - - - - ing;   O

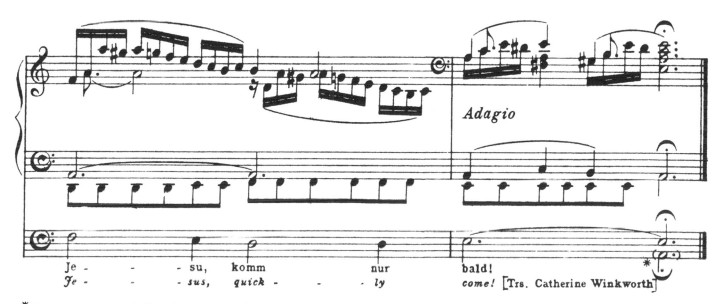

Je - - su, komm   nur   bald!
Je - - sus, quick - ly   come! [Trs. Catherine Winkworth]

*It is recommended that the lower pedal note be omitted here.

No. 11. O Welt, ich muss dich lassen

O world, I now must leave thee

Un - to the Lord's all -
be - fehl'n in Got - tes

- lov - - - ing
gnäd' - - - ge
hands. [Trs. M.D. Calvocoressi]
Hand.

(16 ft in)

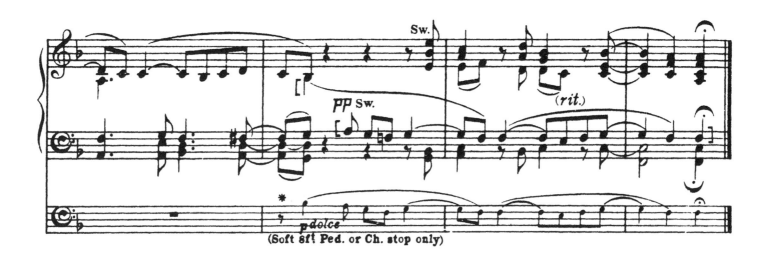

(Soft 8ft Ped. or Ch. stop only)

* The small notes in the Pedal stave should be substituted for the melodic portion of the left hand part placed in brackets, if found practicable.